The One Certain Thing

Books by Peter Cooley

The One Certain Thing

Peter Cooley

Carnegie Mellon University Press
Pittsburgh 2021

Acknowledgments

Certain of these poems or versions of them have appeared, sometimes titled differently in the following magazines, and the author is grateful to the editors for permission to reprint:

The American Journal of Poetry: "Liminalities, a Romance"; *Anglican Theological Review*: "Matins, Evensong"; *Christian Century*: "Barcarolle," "A Strand of Pearls"; *Colorado Review*: "Prime: a Canonical Hour"; *Commonweal*: "Just One of the Afterdeaths," "Étude: October, Falling"; *The Commuter*: "The Two of Us," "First Day of Advent," "An Elegy of Sorts," "Étude: Down-Heaven"; *Copper Nickel*: "The Monkeys, the Monkeys: an Anniversary Poem"; *Crazy Horse*: "Ghost of a Minute"; *Diode*: "Dancer on One Foot"; *Foundry*: "Another of the Stages of Grief"; *Image*: "Visitation: the Eighth Sacrament"; *Lake Effect*: "Beds We Lie In"; *North American Review*: "Widower"; *North Dakota Quarterly*: "A New Orleans Kind of Elegy," "None: The Ninth Canonical Hour"; *On The Seawall*: "Bookish"; *Plume*: "Étude: Not a Sex Poem, "Mythos: a Visitation," "Interrogations Update," "The Color My Sky Always Aspires To" as "Blues Note"; *Peaudunque Review*: "The Dog Next Door and Other Instances"; *Poetry*: "The One Certain Thing"; *Smartish Pace*: "Étude: Rooms We Live and Die In," "Étude: Three-Part Variation on a Loneliness"; *South Florida Poetry Journal*: "Epithalamium," "Apologetics"; *Tiferet*: "You Left Me Your Legacy, Love,"

"Étude: October, Falling" appeared in the anthology *The Slumbering Host*.
"The One Certain Thing" appeared in *American Life In Poetry*, Ted Kooser, Editor.

The author is grateful to Tulane University for a Mellon Professorship which allowed for a number of these poems to be written and to the English Department for additional emotional and financial support.

Thanks to "The Group," Carolyn Hembre, Kay Murphy, Brad Richard, Andy Young, Katie Balma, Rodney Jones, Toi Derricote, Laura Mullen, and Allison Campbell for insightful readings and suggestions.

Thanks as well to Michael Kuczynski, The Reverend James Morrison, Paul Hufnagel, Peter Havholm, Robin Daley, and Lynne Rapp. To Nicole Cooley, Josh Cooley, and Alissa Cooley Rowan special thanks are due for their emotional support and ongoing love.

Book design by Connie Amoroso

in memory of Jacqueline Cooley, 1944 – 2018

Contents

Four

Five

One

"Between grief and nothing, I will take grief."

—William Faulkner, *The Wild Palms*

Widower

There really is no word for it, is there?
"Widower" from "Widow" doesn't say it.
Nothing "says it" except poetry
more crying. I'm not a "widower,"
I was "widowed." And now this imagery,
all I have now, all insufficiency.

This morning when I woke up, you were here,
an indentation in the sheets. You'd left
to start the day in your study, praying.
And, before that, in the middle of the night,
I reached out to touch you or tried to touch—
or was it you, reaching to touch me?

My lines are too interlaced with questioning—

But what else is this hunger not hunger,
thirst not thirst, this aching through my arms,
my legs, how else can I sing with the birds
except to get up before first light again,
to lay my words along, beside, inside
the song that breaks me up, assembles me.

To My Wife, Thirty Days After Her Death

You will not be here to see this spring again,
Love, I counted on our watching—
no, our entering these furious buds
bursting on the magnolias in our yard.
One's just about to open, the white cusp
sprung, now, while we would have watched—

Today I've overslept. I'm awake this minute,
to choose between the two extremities
I'm unprepared to choose.
                                    Shall I begin
the long, deep terrible (no, I'm not ready)
beginning of acceptance that you're not here with me
taking in the long, deep, terrible resurrection buds
or the alternative, the long, deep terrible
nights and days, surrounded by your voice
I'm losing now I'm crying, bringing it back.
And trying to keep you here, putting this down.

First Visitation

When we talk to the dead, they answer or not.
They have that choice. But we don't choose, do we?
Yesterday within the arena of my crying,
I heard your voice, Jacki, gone two months,
but you said—what? I couldn't grasp it.

But then there is the other side, the dead
talking to us through the mire of our unending tasks,
the high wire of the checkbook, circumference of a scrubbed pot
or folding laundry, tangled in unmatched socks,
I catch your voice and now you touch me here
across my right hand, this second, the next.
And as I write this, you're already gone.

You refuse to leave. I'd never ask you to.

Étude: Down-Heaven

How can we love the dead,
when they love us, only eternally?
How can we dare transfix them in a prayer
longing encircles, quickly circumscribes?
When they have ceased to wonder how we are,
occupied as they must be, hourlessly
in a heaven with their new imaginations?

Here, down-heaven in my little fractures,
I try to assemble some facsimile,
Love, of that longing. I try to sound a note—
timpani's symphony. I finish a whole bar.

Even if the smallest of my measures reach you!

And now you surround me, encircling, encircling,
then, taking back your resurrection, disappear.

Ghost of a Moment

When you come back, as you insist these days
on your own terms, a sight unseen, music
I can't hear, a scald across my extended hand
I carry with me, and I can't let go,

it's not to make me long for you. I do
anyway. Your coming makes your leaving,
coming back, a part of me like breathing
after a long run, that heft of body, stinging.

And it assures me I will see our heaven
at noon in all things, star-morning wide,
if I open my eyes—to ours we shared in prayer.
Can this morning really be another

visit to the tomb of Nebuchadnezzar,
the instant Socrates put the hemlock to his lips?
Or when we turn a corner together
in the wind, dazzling, new planet earth?

The Color My Sky Always Aspires To

What color towel will let me cry today
about your sudden death nine months ago?
To bury my face among the tufted hues,

Ambers, ruby-reds, emeralds, amethysts,
Stacking the bathroom cabinet you outfitted?
Last week I wept a solid hour, my face

among the golds. Backcloths were exposed.
Afterwards, the towels in the washer
our second hour, while I cried, a good spin

in the dryer, I was restored. This week
what kind of restoration will today
enact if I'm alone? None. I need this

soft, blue fluff of constellation,
consolation-atta-boys, this heaven,
the color my sky always aspires to,

when I begin. But look, I've started, tears
rush between words, the poem smears and blurs.

Ye Holy Angels Bright

I

Ye holy angels bright, who wait at God's right hand.
When the organ began this, ten o'clock Mass,

breaking broke up again across my wound
I'd stanched and bandaged almost a year now.

That ancient hymn, fresh from your funeral Mass,
you ordered this, forty-one years back

when we heard it, your grandmother's funeral.
"She was my mother," you said, "since my mother

never was a mother." I did just what you asked
But I repeat: the breaking broke in me.

II

That was this morning. Now it's March afternoon,
the sun making random incarnations,

flickering parallels and perpendiculars
a day demands of us, who go on, living.

I've cut the lawn, first pulling dandelions,
their entrance announcing spring is here, early.

Muscling up a sweat drives the hymn out of my head
an hour or so, but now it's back, *Ye Holy—*

Étude: Furnitures of Grief

The teak dresser housing my boxers and your underwear
since you swore we had to own the best, to last,
regardless of our penury at twenty-four, twenty-one.
I need to polish it, a monument.
I don't need all these drawers anymore.

Next the living room couch, plush gray suede
never the same again since I found you,
your tongue hanging at the right side of your mouth.
Love, I touched your forehead. Cold. I knew then.

But the couch squats, a couch and not a couch.
It still takes me, I'm writing this poem now
on the gray cushions, the same gray as your flesh
laid out for fires in the final viewing room.

There's other furniture—our bed, that chair
where you wept months after the baby died.
The rocking chair rocking Josh, now thirty.

No, no, poeticizing! But I'm crying.
I didn't mean to when I started this.

Reading Habits

The sixth month anniversary of your death
I woke up fractured, my body little pieces
as if I'd fallen down a flight of stairs,
my mouth carved out of a cellar space,
my stomach bloated though I was ravenous
yet didn't want to eat, my crying kept coming up,
but eat I had to, chicken noodle soup,
soda crackers, orange jello, diet for the post-operative.

Then I held my head between my palms
as if I could translate the pain ricocheting
into my fingers and transcribe it here.
But I couldn't begin to write a word.

Finally, late afternoon, I fell asleep
reading C. S. Lewis' *Surprised by Joy*,
announcing his conversion, recalling mine,
church gates you led me through
three-quarters of a life ago.

Next day, today, I woke up early
I wasn't sick, that volcano in my soul
quiet and still. So today, only trembling a little.
I went about dusting, your hand over mine
vacuuming—your grip. I wrote another poem,
not this one. I read more C. S. Lewis.
We continued our yesterday, our now,
treading, hours by minutes, our afterlife.

Compline: a Canonical Hour

Our sex? Sure, I miss that, but it's your voice
I crave the most and still can hear right now,
standing beside me as the evening comes,
giving way to darkness between the trees.

I want to hear you share some memory
as you did yesterday, our graveyard—hand-in-hand
when we drove down to New Orleans,
our broken fan belt in Champaign-Urbana,
the car repair shop abutting on these stones.
We danced, we laughed, thirty, thirty-three,
death some quaint inscriptions heft in granite.

Today you're telling me I'm looking good
sporting the orange golf shirt and white pants
you bought me your last months. Did you foresee this day?
I ask: you mean you follow me?

Only sometimes.

There really isn't time here in eternity.

Two

"No one ever told me that grief felt so much like fear. I am not afraid, but the sensation is like being afraid. The same fluttering in the stomach, the same restlessness, the yawning. I keep on swallowing."

—C. S. Lewis, *A Grief Observed*

Smoking, a Romance

Smoking was the postscript to making love
the sixties, seventies, the eighties, for you and me—
maybe all young lovers then?

I never questioned it, the symphony's coda,
the after-dinner drink, I loved the deep
somnambulance that followed, last lines to a song

the two of us wrote, ecstatic melodies.
Then my first friend died of lung cancer,
the second, the next. I wondered why

I had to cough my way across the mornings,
and punctuate the day with cravings,
satiations, cravings, until I quit.

It wasn't easy. But I quit. You kept on,
flying the smoking plane higher, wider.
Coughing, you flew deeper, narrower,

you flew in circles in the smoking plane,
72 cartons of Salems hidden in your study,
the box reading "Taxes 2003"

You coughed the black cough, all night all day.
The penultimate morning of your life
you told me, as if you knew, you'd had one cigarette

the day before. The last day, one-half a cigarette,
The last night I heard no coughing.
In the morning you were dead.

Banality of Grief: a Visitation

This morning I slapped on aftershave to shave,
cupped my left shoe on my right foot,
stashed dirty clothes first in the dryer,
stuck a fork through milk in my cereal.

It didn't continue. Necessities took hold
and when the sun came in, to stand beside my hands
lifted, praying, I knew you would be here, not here
as always now, and by my side, behind me, up ahead.

I'd find you, sitting down to read a poem
I'd just written, maybe even this one,
or maybe not. It may be too flimsy,
the quatrains not quite an appropriate form,

the sonnet it's developing into
not quite right for your eyes, sight twice-alive.

Étude: Rooms We Live and Die In

You told me once: I want to die with you.
It didn't work out. I am still alive,
here in the house we lived in forty years.
I'm naked, walking through the future's furniture
which is our past, the rooms of grief,
grief's curtains you sewed and grief's rugs you bought,
I just got up from sheets of sex and sleep,
the crimson-fitted contours of our bodies—
Yes, I still imagine you beside me.
The crimson-fitted contours of my crying.

I'm crying across the teakwood dresser
extracting my T-shirt, undershorts and socks,
the teak we bought when we had nothing but the future
to pay for it. Twenty-four, twenty-one.

Suddenly, tears won't come. On the east wall
our cross we bought at the Poor Clare's Bazaar,
stares down at me, cheap wood, not His presence
waiting to be crucified, then, crucified,
next, absent, then, risen. He's warped white pine.

The spoon my cereal scoops, part of our wedding set,
comes up to my mouth, an instrument.
The cornflakes taste like carboard, now like cotton.

This is just another morning—are you listening?

Vespers: a Canonical Hour

The kitchen sink, the stainless steel's gray face
I've scoured into quicksilver, stares back at me.
Both bathroom floors I've scrubbed hospital-white,
doggy style on hands and knees as you instructed.

I'm arranging, rearranging, as you would have it:
the running shoes, each in a corner of my study,
the socks balled on the rug beside our bed,
malodorous black template of male untidiness.

Nine months I told myself you were watching.
I pictured you, nodding approval from the sky.
I couldn't, wouldn't, move beyond clichés of grief.
But now I have let go, you can take new forms,

your voice coiling in mine to answer the phone,
Then to dismiss a robocall politely,
And now you're here, quick, under my hands,
hands that swarmed the warm flesh of your body,

left hand that touched your cold forehead that morning.
Right hand that spreads its fingers on this page.
I am lifting both hands, palms up, across the page.
You are not here. I'm not praying to bring you back.

Jason and the Aluminum Siding

The first month without you, I would break down
crying during chin-ups, squats or sit-ups,
loading the dishwasher, picking up my socks
I dropped beside our bed fifty-two years.

Then robocalls flew in like demon spirits:
senior life insurance offers, expiring soon,
threats to cancel my paid-up credit cards,
most of all Jason, the calculated dumb-fuck.

I counted on his song. But what was he selling?
Oh, yes, aluminum siding for "your family home."
My House now, I shouted when he called.

Jason, you moron! I yelled every time.
Jason, what were you but a cracked baritone,
someone to spit-curse, dialogues at high noon
conducted with myself, wild elegies.

The golden fleece was, "Hey, there! This is Jason!"
How is it a robocall, that tremolo I'd anticipate,
could take my loss and, never answering back,
expunge my sobbing, start out to stanch my grief?

You Left Me Your Legacy, Love,

this drawer of multicolored socks, all scored
with painters, Chagall's couple midair,
Van Gogh's cypresses churning, Cezanne's

sheened apples, so I can walk in wonder
every step. You left me my kind of belief,
art's pretense of immortality, an eternity

daily reflection of your faith in heaven.
But why does Seurat's pointillism afternoon
resist a mate unless it's "Echo of a Scream"?

This woman likes a mermaid staring back
while I slip Matisse on my left foot,
now my right, crossing my legs, she'll be here

all day, when I sit down, presence of you.

This Wind, That Wind, a Romance

Because we married young
we didn't know the wind that carried us
so long as we kept faith
in its velocities we had no name for.

We didn't know the wind raised stones.
We didn't know it changed direction with warning.
It carried little stings, it tore off skin, layers of skin
our expectations crying for integument.

We rode these patches, together,
apart. We sometimes couldn't tell the difference.

We turned on each other, tearing.
Which was our skin, which the fabrications?

After a time, they were interchangeable.

We turned back, we burned,
our dance the dance wind orchestrated.

Now I'm alone, with dark inside my hand.

The wind comes certain mornings, others not.
You come to me in visitation or you don't.

Good days the light stands in our wind
blinding. I see by that blindness.
It's in not-seeing that I see you're here with me.

The wind carries, the wind disports and plays.

I don't see you anymore, exactly.
You're always here with me.
This is what I prayed for and the wind granted.
The wind says yes. I asked. It answered, the wind said yes.

Étude: You Must Change Your Life

Though none or few have read Rilke,
the well-meaners or mean-wellers tell me
I must change my life, get a girlfriend,
someone younger, sixty, fifty, forty—
a neighbor I liked until yesterday,
who walks his dog each evening, praising my lawn,
pronounces, "a twenty-year old, Peter, for the challenge."

Others, busy with my newfound retirement
of freedom or boredom, as they perceive it,
every diagnosis a register of their own malaise,
suggest a move to the Lakefront in New Orleans,
site of Katrina devastation, or permanence in New Jersey,
Missouri, California, where our grown children live,
all of them busy, busy, busy, busy.
I could drive kids to their lessons,
do yardwork. Dust? Cook for everyone.

But there is loneliness and there is solitude.
From solitude come agons I have written you,
these grief poems, and I have hours and days
when I can't eat or want to trowel ice cream
out of the carton while watching the soaps and Dr. Phil
or surf the internet for a new car,
another friend's suggestion to slake grief.

Most days I go on surviving with your presence.
Every decision I make I must check with you.
Evenings as I read, here you are, across from me.

You told me to write this. "Make it a light poem,
comic relief." All right, I'm doing that.
Now I'm going to write an agon. Now read the Gospel for today.

Apologetics

Christ of the only world I know today
risen for me, splayed sunshine on the floor,
why do I have to wake up the same man,
same body I woke in yesterday?

But since You only speak to me in *my* words,
breaking out images to concoct a poem,
or in the silences between the lines,
and this is not a poem yet, I'm searching,

questioning, while You wait in the dust motes—

This is the body I was born to die in.
I wipe the night away from cheeks and forehead.
Another cup of coffee, then a poem?
Silence, my Christ, my answers are all questions.

Three

"There is a time when death is an event, an adventure, and as such mobilizes, interests, activates, tetanizes. And then one day it is no longer an event, it is another *duration*, compressed, insignificant, not narrated, grim, without recourse; true mourning not susceptible to any narrative dialectic."

—Roland Barthes, *Mourning Diary*

Mythos: a Visitation

You must begin to die into your life
the morning said, but since morning only speaks
like poetry in specificities,
it was the trees that spoke,
the trees along my street this morning run,
half of it ambling, their language demotic,
the roots spread out across the world.

Have you learned nothing from your wife's death
eight months back? the live oak asks
followed in chorus by the sweet olive and willow.
I don't answer. I don't need to.

I must begin again as the sun begins
to see these steps a dance I've never danced
while the enchantment lasts, the trees speaking.
It will play, as always, a few seconds.

That's how the eons turn, the sun said.
Then the trees were silent, each step transformation—

First Day of Advent

Our Advent calendar, crimson edging
green felt, you sewed twenty-five years back,
waits to be hung up. I have to stop crying.

Little pockets number days until Christ's birth,
each holding a hook. I have to stop crying.
I'll loop a star on everyone as the days come on.

I have to stop crying. That day together
we hung this calendar where I will fix it soon
by the front window. Until Christ's birth.

You sewed these pieces, you complained.
"Why do it?" I shot back. I have to stop
crying. We started quarreling after that.

Only sex could fix it. I. Have. To. Stop.
That crying day you put this in my hands
to tack up in gold light. Christ's birth.

Stop crying. I have the first star here
in my right hand. Christ's birth. Our window's gold!
We couldn't stop crying that day—both of us—

until we made love. The star glistens, holds
my stare. It steadies, years on fire, here.
Christ's birth, the star glistens, gold. The window,

the stars, trade faces. Transfigurations.
Twenty-five years. The first day of Advent.
I have to stop, I have to stop crying.

Visitation: the Dog Next Door and Other Instances

I told the first birds, who had awakened me,
 too busy singing to listen, but they knew.
Reader, taking this in? No, a few more examples.
The friend's cat on my lap, wise enough to doze

midafternoon so she can mouse all night.
She knows. But do my friend and I?
Reader, won't you admit you share with me
a belief in immortality of the flesh

while we're healthy, as I am, and I hope you are.
Maybe later, immortality of the soul?
The dog next door howls to start the day,
he knows, a kingly German Shepherd.

They all know what I can't get or bear to get
just yet, the animal fact of death.

Étude: Blues

Today I gave away your winter clothes.
You will not face another January
beside me, pull up the scrim of the ice-blue parka hood
against the wind, a skin I'm still maneuvering,
my mother, father, sister, aunt,
grandmother, grandfather wind. All my dead.

Ice blue. The color of your tongue that morning
I found you, splaying the living room couch
after you left our bed, your back on fire,
stenosis claiming your spine, your shoulders, arms.

A corresponding blue this raincoat, too,
a shade deeper, a London Fog we bought
in London on a whim since we were Londoning
and knew the price inflated just for us.
How could we not indulge in such a blue?

Tomorrow I'll gave away your spring clothes,
then summer's lush pastels, and then your fall's.
Why do I tell myself I can diminish
even for a second this soul's wounding's blue
bruising my legs, my shoulder blades, my arms?

The Monkeys, the Monkeys: an Anniversary Poem

Our days come so they may go away.
We have so many-few, and who can stop to count?

This sounds like the beginning of a villanelle!
No, no, I want pentameter to stop!

There, I've stanched it.
On the morning dresser, the mourning

dresser, down the dawn-blue
first light, two little monkeys

I bought you at the eponymous coffee shop.
One gold-gray, in imitation

of my graying, the other the color
(I see I fall into pentameter

by habit!) your hair kept, the auburn hue
that poet referenced in "The Nut-Brown Maid."

The monkeys intertwine.
Did I lay them out that way?

Did you, before I found you—
in the identical blue-dawn light

a year ago today—
splayed on the couch,

your tongue hung across your lower lip?
I knew before I touched your cold forehead—

rhyme lets me say it. And pentameter.

I knew you were dead.

Liminalities, a Romance

Our priest maintains you have gone to be with God,
I have to let you go. I know I'm not ready,
occupied daily with the momentaries
I find in our house we shared forty years.

These afghans you crocheted—I watch your hands
working the blue one I'm picking up,
It's my hands crocheting: I don't know how.

Yarn flies back into the tangled dark,
the bin I pulled it from. You're not anywhere

I am. This instant, at the window, gold prepares
entrance to our bedroom. I pull the curtain. Come back.

Étude: Three-Part Variation on a Loneliness

I

Today I couldn't give away certain books we owned,
front covers where we had glued in "Ex Libris" and our names—
Wuthering Heights, Madame Bovary, The Complete Shakespeare—
you're listening, aren't you? Onto the toppling pile

teetered *The Faerie Queen, Sampson Agonistes,*
Hemingway's Poems, The Compleate Angler.
Remember how I bought that? You shook your head,
"Another of your dumb whims." Right again.

II

I have my mornings when I'm sure you're here,
alive, waking beside me, your hand splayed across my chest,
but they are fewer now. When I come home
I'm used to being greeted before I enter
by The Loneliness, an emptiness I stomp on.

III

Most days you are with me like another finger,
another toe, to help me grasp or stumble
without falling, grappling, righting myself.

You keep me passing through the immovables.

You, a touch grazing my arm—both of us have put here.
We pretend you're still alive. Both of us together, lying.

Remember you said once you would go to the end
of the earth for me? Is that where we are now?

Epidermal: a Visitation

I've just put on, donned, the royal purple robe
you sewed for me—how many years, back, forty?
You always bought the most expensive fabrics.
I don't know names of cloth. Egyptian cotton?

I just know the purple hasn't faded.
I just know I'm slipping on your skin
assuming this. It molds my shoulders.
Your ligaments hold my arms, fixed, writing us.

I yank the sash loosely around my waist.

Why pray the prayers of the first year's grief,
for the relief of twisting in my stomach,
back and legs and thighs racked, spasming,
when I have this purple king's gown around me?

Halfway now through the second year you're here
you're back, you're standing with me, second skin,
as our children are, wearing us right now.

They're waking up, they stretch, they yawn,
in their three different states. They're wearing us.
Maybe they know that. Maybe they just assume it.

I pull the robe's sash tight. I tie the purple knot.

Spirit Ground, a Romance

I knew you as I know myself, daily,
as I love and hate myself, the twitches
down my shoulder mornings, my rib spasms,
the scab on my left knee—or is it yours?

The molar where you/I can't bite down hard.

Our love of "The River Merchant's Wife"
you introduced me to; spearmint frozen yogurt;
Wuthering Heights, our favorite novel when we met;

the light between trees wind gathers into a fist:
I showed you what that stood for, I took your hand
to walk years with me under the canopy,
the branches enfolding transfiguration light.

You taught me it was spirit ground we traveled.

I think you're writing this with me, aren't you?
Slip your fingers over mine. Steady my hand.

This Didn't Happen, It Could Happen

If I tell you I am like the husband in "Neighbors,"
the Raymond Carver story, donning women's clothes,
say that I put on my wife's, my dead wife's from this cache
I was saving for the Salvation Army,
what would you think? Blouse, skirt, underwear.

I loved her in the Valentine-red blouse
I bought her, black underwear so skimpy
it was hardly there for me to peel off,
see-through fishnet. I loved her in her teal blue blouse
of her own purchase. I could have donned them all.
I could say I allowed this house, the widower's,
to take in my full display. Would I embarrass you?

I didn't do this. I pulled out the Carver story,
reread, reread. I recommend you look at it.

I may still put on the clothes. They're safe
next to T-shirts, boxers, in a drawer we shared.
But I think all the clothes might be too tight
for me to write a decent poem about this.

Four

"The power of grief to derange the mind has in fact been exhaustively
noted. The act of grieving, Freud told us in his 1917 'Mourning and
Melancholy,' 'involves grave departures from the normal attitude to
life.' Yet, he pointed out, grief remains peculiar among derangements.
'It never occurs to us to regard it as a pathological condition and to
refer it to medical treatment.' We rely instead on 'its being overcome
after a certain lapse of time.'"

—Joan Didion, *The Year of Magical Thinking*

Barcarolle

The day I was confirmed, you turned to me,
sang out, while I stared straight ahead
through the sudden Wisconsin blizzard,

trying to keep our car on course toward home,
"Maybe this is why we got together."
I thought that was too much hindsight, foresight.

Now, ten months into your death, our life
together winds and unwinds, spiraling,
snow drifting, melting, freezing to melt again.

On the west wall of the room you smoked in,
coughed through, smoked, room I've had repainted
that blue the sky aspires to, our cross

we bought together at the convent's Christmas bazaar,
our cross holds up these words you've brought to me.
Hanging it back up in the repainted room,

after the fumigation and new blue,
I chipped the paint, the plaster. The cross—
it waits for me to finish singing this. The cross—

the cross is still not finished with us yet.
The cross stares down at me, a still, unfinished look.

Secrets of the Keys, a Romance

Among the few pieces of jewelry
I excavated from a single box—
your engagement pearls, the antique locket
I gifted you one Christmas and where you glued
a photo of our children with me opposite—
I found two keys I'd never seen.

I pulled them out, laid them across our bed,
over the mottled bedspread where the sky
at the east window came and went and came,
the rhythm blue, improvisational.

A jailor's turnkey, silver, palm sized.
The second corroded green and purple.
Dumbly, I tried both keys on the front door,
the back, even my car, the ancient desk
you bought me with its lock I've never locked.

I pulled on my jogging suit, the black and white
you gifted me, then said I was a panda,
a penguin, remember? The both of us,
doubled up. Why did you die? I'll never know, will I?

I ran, I ran to the river, my restless friend,
the Mississippi taking its own course
below the levee, the end of our street.
Corroded, green, the obstreperous,
polluted, open-jawed stupor of the tides,
stupor of the purple skies reflected there,
readied themselves. They've taken in everything.
I thought about the two of us, what I'll never know.
Then hurled both sets of keys in the water.

This Living Hand: a Visitation

—after Keats

My cross entangled in your cross this morning
when I pulled then both off my neck to shower.
I've been disentangling them an hour now.

You gifted me my cross, I gave you yours,
mine when I was baptized and confirmed at thirty,
yours for our 50th anniversary.

Before they took your body to be burned
I scooped yours from your neck (no one was there
in the laying-out room to catch this rite),
slipped it on mine. Nine months they've hung together.

Entangling, disentangling. Obvious!
I wasn't going to write this. It's no poem.
Maybe it's just you, speaking to me again.

moving my living hand across the page,
touching, slipping apart, skimming mortal day.

Epithalamium

The trees keep telling me we're only passing through,
the live oaks of New Orleans City Park.
"But legend says we stood here before Christ."

Under the boughs of summer, I am wandering again,
no end in sight, watched over by that sun
darkening at the hour of the crucifixion.
Here in the Park, my five white swans, one black,
split the lagoon's dark mirror, all their grace
disguising awkwardness. If I should shout
as shout I have, I won't today, the black
could be new image of the afterlife,
an immortality.
                    I have only to ask.

Étude: Dancer on One Foot

All my friends are dead, my aunt said, her late eighties.
At seventy-seven, I'm treading down her path:
Tom, Linda, Raquel, Fred, Elmer, Dorothy,
Jacki, my wife, me, a dinner party the mid '70s.
And only me still here.
                    Therefore, I will inscribe
these few lines about the morning at my feet,
insistence of the sun on following me around.

The east windows are tabernacle-bright,
every pane another frieze of gold.
But it's the light down here, hopping, uninvited,
the one-legged bird with a shriveled wing—
this is my follower who makes me follow him,
who dances on one foot, rehearsing joy,
who flies across the skies I've never seen,
the cloud-cover he travels on the floor.

His light is the discovery of old age,
possibilities, dark shining in everything.

Bibliomania, a Romance

Will I really be dust like these clotted puffs
my cloth wipes from the top of the bookcase,
floats downwards to the shelves, Akhmatova,

Apollinaire, Bishop, Cavafy, Donne?
Only a little on their tops, less on their sides.
Only a very little dust across their names.

I'm on the next shelf now. Glück, Hopkins, Kinnell.
Louise the living, the other two dust, dust.
Only a very little across their names.

Outside, my Monday rushes forward,
a world hurtling to self-destruct.
I have to take my place in it by nine o'clock.

But in here light quickens around the dust.
I have so many shelves to finish before I go,
fiction, nonfiction, biography, art, religion.

The dust continues, Lowell, Merwin, Moore.
Only a little on their tops, less on their sides.
Only a very little across their names.

Dust on my cloth, dust you have turned to,
after the fires, dust I can never touch
inside the stone. Your name there, Jacki, waiting for mine.

Hardscrabble

Christ between us as I put down these words,
Over us, behind, ahead, every whichway,
the nighttime in my room a part of Him.

Yes, that darkness, its deep clarity.

Christ is that midnight. He breaks it as I speak.
Love, He has brought you here to witness this.
While you were alive, He moved—through us.

How else could we have mended, broken, mended

our hardscrabble steps fifty-two years?
When I bring you back or you appear
of your own volition, Christ's beside you.

Then He moves off so we can talk and talk.

While I've been writing this, you have been leaving.
The day awaits, the sky is a white page.
The day awaits, surprise its agency.

He's gone, He's here, like you, He goes and comes.
Are you waiting to see me—as Christ insists?

Étude: the Golden Hour

I'm sitting here, the couch's window side
where I'd find you when I'd slumped through the door
for dinner, exhaustion in my grip
etching the lifelines. Or sometimes joy burst in
accompanying a favorite bouquet for you,
the cheap daisies lasting weeks with your finesse.

We've all heard stories of the dog who waits
years by the door for an owner to come back.
The spaniel of my friend's dead father waited a year,
and at the end, refusing food, died overnight.
Love, that isn't us. Love, Love, Love, come—
and now, on time, your presence, the golden hour,

this passing fixing one second to the next—

A Strand of Pearls

A single lamentation, I'm done?
No, just a different one, to name the rains,

tintinnabulation at the window,
the bent lament of morning's radiance

refusing to appear at this blue glass
where last night I could reach out, name the stars,

many, many my imaginations.
Where are the pearls you wore for your engagement photo

watching me from the piano as I pass by,
piano you played until the end, even half-blind?

These pearls—the girl who wore them stands right now
beside me, mere seconds, in this prayer-poem.

Seconds. God, the cruelty of prayer.

Columbarium

I Front

After Mass, every Sunday in the churchyard
I've come to visit you, touch the weatherings
along the roseate stone carved with your name,
birthdate, death date. Then with my fingertips
I drop a kiss along the façade—and you're inside.

II Sides

Sometimes my fingers slip, I brush my waiting place
below or next to you, I'm not sure which.
"That check includes you, too, Peter," Father Jim said,
his faith in immortality, melodious, commodious,
monotonous concerto for violin and cello.

III Back

You're no more there than are here,
where, when, I go to find you, these revenants
haunting the top drawer of the dresser.
Multicolored underwear I bought you holidays,
those pearls caught in your engagement picture.

IV Top

Next Sunday, maybe, I'll skip a visit.
Why try to find you when you're always
Shadow and light intertwined beside me,
day-night, sun-moon, their syncopations
unasked for, random grace I can't answer.

Five

"There is another world and it is in this one."

—Paul Éluard

Prime: a Canoncial Hour

After this life I'm waking to,
I will certainly be back again, won't I?
I know I have been here before, and countlessly.
This life—my irises and pupils prehensile,
poised to strike, open the widening day.

Can it really be this morning dove
sequestered predawn in the neighbor's yard,
plangent agony, taut, inexpressible
in words, known only in breaking, breaking
me, to reassemble me, to break—

can it be, Father, I come to premonitions
of the before life, the afterlife, each morning?
Yes, if I listen, wounding music
healing, wounding as it sings.

Mother of the Risen God, is this Who I think It is?

Étude: Not a Sex Poem

My body over your body, skin on skin.
I go on missing that inseparability,
yes, the soul-trading in our bodying.

But it's the grazing touch, walking beside you,
falling asleep, your hand across my chest,
that hand and then my own, moving across it,

living in the warm flesh, exchanging that touch.
That's what I can't bring back. These words are cold,
substitute music, substitute imagery.

Today putting this down awakens nothing in me.
(I wrote a sex poem about us. I tore it up.)
Father Jim repeated yesterday again

we'll be together forever when my ashes
find their place beside you in that granite vault.
He repeats I will see you instantly

on the other side. Today I should believe him.
I can't, I can't. I touch this page,
you're not here, you're not anywhere.

Today I'll make you up again in words
I write across the wind. The wind knows us.
The wind has taken me in, moments, years, like this.

Interrogations Update

When will I see you again? I've asked the priests.
Father Jim says when I die, that exact instant.
Father Jonathan now, in these visitations,
when I see you cross the living room
in the scarlet nightgown I gave you last Christmas.
You're here and somewhere else, he claims,
referring me to Wikipedia,
the garbled entry on quantum physics,
"A body in two places at the same time."
Father Dave: at the end of time. Father Ted:
When we rise again, every one of us.
When is that? I ask. He shrugs. A mystery.

Why do I keep questioning when you're here, now,
your presence in our shadowed room the sun,
appearing, reappearing this very second?

Outside, thunderheads assemble a December.
The light in our bedroom comes and goes, spilling
golds on the familiars of our life together—
ancient bed, teak dressers we couldn't afford
but bought anyway to stay the course. Half a century.
The rocking chair my grandmother embroidered
with moons and stars, where you'd lay out your clothes
for morning every night. I take that darkness-light,
I hold it with both hands. It's everything,
everything of you I get to keep.

Community of Grief, a Romance

My first grief group was the morning trees.
When I went out at dawn to give them my weeping
they listened and responded, shaking leaves,
limbs the wind shook into tintinnabulation,
these legendary live oaks of New Orleans.

And in the music of that listening I was lifted?

Then two of my oldest friends, now in their seventies
both lost their wives like me, the vines snapped suddenly.
We crossed the limbos among us on the internet.
Today we live in the same country of soul-woundings.

Then the church grief group, counselor, priest,
the five of us, I the only male,
the brother's suicide by hanging, the sister's rare
lymphoma at twenty-one, our counselor
encouraging us to weep, our priest to pray,
quoting Christ to Lazarus, *Awake, awake!*
the music of that resurrection thundering.

Now these words of mine, offered to the winds—

Matins, Evensong

I find you every morning in my prayers.
All night you have been waiting, haven't you?
When I begin "Our Father," you appear.
You stand beside me as the words splay out.
You'll stay till the St. Francis prayer winds up.

All day while I am occupied otherwise
you're by my side, but I don't think of you
except as I think of my feet. They carry me.
As I think of my hands. They reach and grip.
Your eyes in mine go out to round the world,
releasing its peripherals. It's you or God
standing inside invisibilities—
or Christ, asking of me the impossible
since you can't. When He leaves,
it's His words, here, wonderments, my answer.

Étude: October, Falling

Last night the trees changed color while I slept.
One moment at my window: transfigurations.
Love, do you continue transmuting where you are?

Pandemonium of the color wheel. That raucousness.
Noise the sky can hear I call October falling.
Now, outside, calling you to join me, Love,

I kick the leaf piles wind has prearranged.
This is what I want to do with my seventies,
honor sky, scatter stained glass on the sidewalk,

follow the path variegations take us, you beside me.
Then, befriend the wind I'd call an enemy,
flatter it a little with the truth.

Wind, you have a longer history than my breath
encircling worlds before they could take shape,
arranging, disarranging, misaligning to align—

Visitation: the Eighth Sacrament

Now I have days I never think of you
just as my shrink predicted. Milestones pass,
the eighth-month anniversary, the next,
disappearing like thunderheads across the gulf.

But your presences, Love, center my feet
this morning, running, again around the block.
Now you are a monotonousness, of grace-
light under my steps, the unseen seen,

leading me, winded back to our own house.
You're there, you're here, you are this sacrament
only the grieving know, together with the grieved.

Which one of us is writing this? Me? You?
Why, both, of course, inspired by the light
When dawn throws down its crowns, the blinding luminous,

shaping the fractured world into unbrokenness.

Soundings

I

Now-morning-wide, I find myself in stars
making processional disappearances.
Not even one can light me through the hours.
They have offices some other hemisphere.

II

Last night you were here, countlessness,
scintillance, brilliance, an arc to number me
my days until I'm with you, as our priest insists:
I'll see you the millisecond I leave earth.

But now I see myself smallest of stars
in some constellation our three children
imagine.

III

(One star in that darkness
    sustains an immortality)

IV

                One heaven
ensnares a multitude of heavens,
one dissonance a harmony, one note
this moment, I tell myself I've found you,

V

agony between asking and answer.

Letter to God, Letter to Jacki, a Romance

Watch over my love in her paradise,
Lord, until you bring me into my own.

Meanwhile, there is the one I live down here:
Wind pinked by the magnolia trees' first light

as I go out, walking with February,
the sudden trees cathedral spires—

false spring between bud and blossoming.

Love, this is a day you're watching me,
I tell myself. (Some days I know you can't,

you're too busy.) And even though you wait
for me "at home" and accompany my steps

only in my recounting, you're happy
I'm living in this present with a springtime

of trees, limbs stretching me out, between bud
and blossoming, some rare air's aria.

None: the Ninth Canonical Hour

Now, graced, I'm finding us in this old couple
together, the hospital lobby. I've just returned
from my annual checkup, the tests results
witness to my continuing good luck.

While you were living, I couldn't see myself
"old," just "aging" beside you as we processed.
When I looked at you, even at seventy,
bent by spinal stenosis, I saw me,
twenty-four, beside you, twenty-one.

They're aging as I gawk. They can't get up.
They're watching for the van to the old folks home
called "assisted living" even by them.
They're bending to rise, together now.
He tries, courtly, to help her don her coat.
They're standing, wobbly, steps mincing the trek
toward outside, our clear December awaiting us.

They're heading for the door, the outside.
She's on his arm. It's him she's holding up.

No, they hold each other up. Sentimental.

Just One of the Afterdeaths

Returning from the first eternity
I glimpsed when they handed me her ashes,

to the eternal moment where we live,
I saw rendings stitching up themselves

in the live oaks lightning-bent, which would not break,
in scattering of the azaleas' blossoms

from our false spring returned to winter's snap,
and then turned back to spring and blossoming.

Whatever vow I made yesterdays' gods
won't get me through this morning's lacerations . . .

There's honey in the wind, my first god sings,
a god hidden, as all sprits remain

.until we call them in our desperations.
All right, I'm putting in that call. Now, here,

the corners of the hours, call-and-response
poured through the streets' fissures when I look down,

starting my prayers on their morning walk,

First Canonical Hour, Last Interrogation

I

When will the star I prayed to as a child
rise from the concrete sidewalk of prayer
to watch over my stumblings, murmurs, starts,
restarts, to be reborn, like the sun?

This prayer has no circumference, only a churning, dead-white center.

II

Never question why day rises through the trees
the back of my yard, to set, golden, in the front,
then pass on, lighting the other sides of our world.

III

In memory of that gold when I reach out—
even though the scorch across my fist
tells me I should not be resisting,
I resist, then surrender and open, wide—

it happens, happenstance which is not that
but miracles-on-miracle of incarnation—

gold pencils on my desk, gold desk, chair gold,
computer gold, with a light inside this moment
I can't count while it lasts. And it's still here—

The One Certain Thing

A day will come I'll watch you reading this.
I'll look up from these words I'm writing now—
this line I'm standing on. I'll be right here,
alive again. I'll breathe on you this breath.
Touch this word now, that one. Warm, isn't it?

You are the person come to clean my room;
you are whichever one of my three children
opens the drawer here where this poem will go
in a few minutes when I've had my say.

These are the words from immortality.
No one stands between us now except Death:
I enter it entirely writing this.
I have to tell you I am not alone.
Watching you read, Eternity's with me.
We like to watch you read. Read us again.

2007
Trick Pear, Suzanne Cleary
So I Will Till the Ground, Gregory Djanikian
Black Threads, Jeff Friedman
Drift and Pulse, Kathleen Halme
The Playhouse Near Dark, Elizabeth Holmes
On the Vanishing of Large Creatures, Susan Hutton
One Season Behind, Sarah Rosenblatt
Indeed I Was Pleased with the World, Mary Ruefle
The Situation, John Skoyles

2008
The Grace of Necessity, Samuel Green
After West, James Harms
Anticipate the Coming Reservoir, John Hoppenthaler
Convertible Night, Flurry of Stones, Dzvinia Orlowsky
Parable Hunter, Ricardo Pau-Llosa
The Book of Sleep, Eleanor Stanford

2009
Divine Margins, Peter Cooley
Cultural Studies, Kevin A. González
Dear Apocalypse, K. A. Hays
Warhol-o-rama, Peter Oresick
Cave of the Yellow Volkswagen, Maureen Seaton
Group Portrait from Hell, David Schloss
Birdwatching in Wartime, Jeffrey Thomson

2010
The Diminishing House, Nicky Beer
A World Remembered, T. Alan Broughton
Say Sand, Daniel Coudriet
Knock Knock, Heather Hartley
In the Land We Imagined Ourselves, Jonathan Johnson
Selected Early Poems: 1958-1983, Greg Kuzma
The Other Life: Selected Poems, Herbert Scott
Admission, Jerry Williams

2011

Having a Little Talk with Capital P Poetry, Jim Daniels
Oz, Nancy Eimers
Working in Flour, Jeff Friedman
Scorpio Rising: Selected Poems, Richard Katrovas
The Politics, Benjamin Paloff
Copperhead, Rachel Richardson

2012

Now Make an Altar, Amy Beeder
Still Some Cake, James Cummins
Comet Scar, James Harms
Early Creatures, Native Gods, K. A. Hays
That Was Oasis, Michael McFee
Blue Rust, Joseph Millar
Spitshine, Anne Marie Rooney
Civil Twilight, Margot Schilpp

2013

Oregon, Henry Carlile
Selvage, Donna Johnson
At the Autopsy of Vaslav Nijinksy, Bridget Lowe
Silvertone, Dzvinia Orlowsky
Fibonacci Batman: New & Selected Poems (1991-2011), Maureen Seaton
When We Were Cherished, Eve Shelnutt
The Fortunate Era, Arthur Smith
Birds of the Air, David Yezzi

2014

Night Bus to the Afterlife, Peter Cooley
Alexandria, Jasmine Bailey
Dear Gravity, Gregory Djanikian
Pretenders, Jeff Friedman
How I Went Red, Maggie Glover
All That Might Be Done, Samuel Green
Man, Ricardo Pau-Llosa
The Wingless, Cecilia Llompart

2015
The Octopus Game, Nicky Beer
The Voices, Michael Dennis Browne
Domestic Garden, John Hoppenthaler
We Mammals in Hospitable Times, Jynne Dilling Martin
And His Orchestra, Benjamin Paloff
Know Thyself, Joyce Peseroff
cadabra, Dan Rosenberg
The Long Haul, Vern Rutsala
Bartram's Garden, Eleanor Stanford

2016
Something Sinister, Hayan Charara
The Spokes of Venus, Rebecca Morgan Frank
Adult Swim, Heather Hartley
Swastika into Lotus, Richard Katrovas
The Nomenclature of Small Things, Lynn Pedersen
Hundred-Year Wave, Rachel Richardson
Where Are We in This Story, Sarah Rosenblatt
Inside Job, John Skoyles
Suddenly It's Evening: Selected Poems, John Skoyles

2017
Disappeared, Jasmine V. Bailey
Custody of the Eyes, Kimberly Burwick
Dream of the Gone-From City, Barbara Edelman
Sometimes We're All Living in a Foreign Country, Rebecca Morgan Frank
Rowing with Wings, James Harms
Windthrow, K. A. Hays
We Were Once Here, Michael McFee
Kingdom, Joseph Millar
The Histories, Jason Whitmarsh

2018
World Without Finishing, Peter Cooley
May Is an Island, Jonathan Johnson
The End of Spectacle, Virginia Konchan

Big Windows, Lauren Moseley
Bad Harvest, Dzvinia Orlowsky
The Turning, Ricardo Pau-Llosa
Immortal Village, Kathryn Rhett
No Beautiful, Anne Marie Rooney
Last City, Brian Sneeden
Imaginal Marriage, Eleanor Stanford
Black Sea, David Yezzi

2019
Brightword, Kimberly Burwick
The Complaints, W. S. Di Piero
Ordinary Chaos, Kimberly Kruge
Mad Tiny, Emily Pettit
Afterswarm, Margot Schilpp

2020
Build Me a Boat, Michael Dennis Browne
Sojourners of the In-Between, Gregory Djanikian
The Marksman, Jeff Friedman
Disturbing the Light, Samuel Green
Any God Will Do, Virginia Konchan
My Second Work, Bridget Lowe
Flourish, Dora Malech
Petition, Joyce Peseroff
Take Nothing, Deborah Pope

2021
The One Certain Thing, Peter Cooley
The Knives We Need, Nava EtShalom
Oh You Robot Saints!, Rebecca Morgan Frank
Dark Harvest: New & Selected Poems, 2001-2020, Joseph Millar
Glorious Veils of Diane, Rainie Oet
Yes and No, John Skoyles